Brands We Know

Google

By Sara Green

Bellwether Media • Minneapolis, MN

Jump into the cockpit and take flight with Pilot books. Your journey will take you on high-energy adventures as you learn about all that is wild, weird, fascinating, and fun!

This edition first published in 2016 by Bellwether Media, Inc.

No part of this publication may be reproduced in whole or in part without written permission of the publisher.
For information regarding permission, write to Bellwether Media, Inc.,
Attention: Permissions Department,
5357 Penn Avenue South, Minneapolis, MN 55419.

Library of Congress Cataloging-in-Publication Data

Names: Green, Sara, 1964- author.
Title: Google / by Sara Green.
Description: Minneapolis, MN : Bellwether Media, Inc., [2016] | Series:
  Pilot: Brands We Know | Includes bibliographical references and index.
Identifiers: LCCN 2015029932 | ISBN 9781626173477 (hardcover : alk.
paper)
Subjects: LCSH: Google (Firm)--Juvenile literature. | Google--Juvenile
  literature. | Internet industry--United States--Juvenile literature.
Classification: LCC HD9696.8.U64 G66527 2016 | DDC
338.7/61025040973--dc23
LC record available at http://lccn.loc.gov/2015029932

Printed in the United States of America, North Mankato, MN.

Google

Table of Contents

What Is Google?

A student is typing a report about the planet Saturn. Google will help! She goes to Google's home page and enters "Saturn" in the search bar. In an instant, Google offers a list of results from the **web**. The student learns that Saturn is the second-largest planet in the solar system. Google makes finding this information easy.

Today, Google Inc., also called Google, is a technology leader. Its **headquarters** is in Mountain View, California. In addition to its **search engine**, Google provides many other services and products. These include Gmail, a popular email service, and Android, a mobile **operating system**. Another favorite product is a **web browser** called Google Chrome. For directions, many people rely on Google Maps. Companies also use Google to **advertise** products. In 2015, Google was worth more than $360 billion! This makes it one of the most valuable **brands** on Earth.

By the Numbers

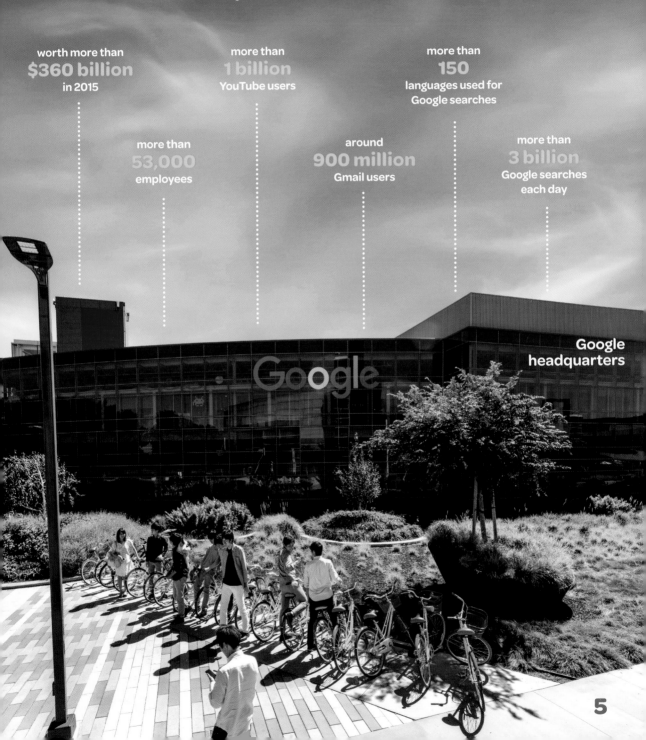

worth more than
$360 billion
in 2015

more than
1 billion
YouTube users

more than
150
languages used for
Google searches

more than
53,000
employees

around
900 million
Gmail users

more than
3 billion
Google searches
each day

**Google
headquarters**

A Team Effort

Google began as a research project. **Founders** Larry Page and Sergey Brin met in 1995 at Stanford University in Palo Alto, California. They both studied computer science. Larry was researching the web. Sergey's focus was **data mining**. They shared an interest in how computers give people information. Soon, the two became friends. They decided to work together to learn how web sites were connected.

Within a year, they had built a search engine called BackRub. It used **backlinks** to rank the importance of web sites. People all over campus wanted to use it! Larry and Sergey later named their search engine "Google" after the mathematical term **googol**. This is the number one followed by a hundred zeros. The name represents the massive amount of information on the web.

Look It Up

In 2006, the verb "google" was added to the *Oxford English Dictionary*. It means to conduct a web search.

To organize the world's information and make it universally accessible and useful

Google mission statement

Larry Page

Sergey Brin

Googleplex

The search engine's success inspired Larry and Sergey. They put their PhD degrees on hold to further develop Google. In 1998, Larry and Sergey moved to Menlo Park, California. There, they launched their company, Google Inc. Larry became the **CEO** and Sergey was the president. Users around the world loved how quickly the search engine worked. The company rapidly grew!

Soon, Google needed more space. In 1999, the company moved into several buildings in Mountain View, California. By the following year, Google had become the largest search engine in the world. Millions of people were searching on Google every day. The company soon moved to an even bigger headquarters in Mountain View called the "Googleplex."

Doodles
Google Doodles are the fun drawings of Google's logo. They honor days like holidays, anniversaries, or the lives of famous people. More than 2,000 different doodles have been posted on Google's home page over time!

More Than a Search Engine

Google has developed other popular products and services. Gmail is Google's email service. It was launched in 2004. Gmail was one of the first email services to group messages into conversations. Today, around 900 million people worldwide use Gmail. Chrome is also popular. It is Google's web browser. It helps people locate and organize information online.

Google Chrome logo

Gmail

Google Earth ....

Many businesses and schools use an **app** called Google Docs. It allows people to create and share documents online. The documents can be accessed in Google Drive, the company's online storage system. People in different places can work on a project at the same time. Google Earth is another favorite product. Users can explore maps, landscapes, and even outer space! Street View is a popular feature of Google Maps. It gives people a close look at places all over the globe.

In 2005, Google took a big step. It bought a cell phone **software** company called Android. Today, Android software powers more than one billion **tablets** and smartphones. Android users can browse more than one million apps in Google Play, an app store. Google Play also offers books, videos, music, and games for instant use.

G1 Android phone

Sweet Androids

Each Android version is named after a dessert. Cupcake was the first version. It was followed by Donut and Eclair. In 2015, Marshmallow was released. Statues of the desserts are displayed on the Googleplex lawn.

Google also owns YouTube. It bought the popular video-sharing site in 2006. Now, YouTube streams more than 4 billion videos every day. Popular video themes include music, cooking, and pets at play. Almost any subject can be made into a YouTube video.

People can use Google Cardboard to experience **virtual reality**. Google Cardboard has special apps and lenses. These allow users to turn their smartphones into virtual reality viewers. Many apps are being developed so people can do more with Cardboard, like play new games and view art galleries. This will make virtual reality seem even more real!

Google Cardboard

Branching Out

Google started a research lab called Google X in 2010. The lab's purpose is to invent new technologies, such as the self-driving car. A balloon project will give people in remote areas access to the Internet.

In 2015, Larry announced a big change. Google and Google X would become separate companies under a larger company called Alphabet. Larry also revealed other companies now under Alphabet. Life Sciences and Calico both seek ways to help people live healthier lives. Nest makes energy-saving **thermostats** and other safety devices. Another company, Google Fiber, provides Internet service to cities. Two **investment** companies help other technology businesses succeed. Larry is Alphabet's CEO, and Sergey is president. Sundar Pichai now heads Alphabet's biggest company, Google.

Deep-Thinking Machine

Google owns a company called DeepMind. It uses video games to teach computers how to think like humans.

self-driving car

Sundar Pichai

Search Tricks on Google

Search Term	What It Does
Atari Breakout (image search)	Starts a game called Image Breakout
Blink HTML	Flashes the words "blink" and "HTML"
Do a Barrel Roll	Spins the page
Flip a Coin	Flips a coin to land heads or tails
Google in 1998	Makes the page appear as it did in 1998
Play Pac-Man Doodle	Brings up a playable Pac-Man game
Roll a Die	Rolls a six-sided die
Set Timer	Shows a timer to use
Tilt	Tilts the page
Zerg Rush	Drops Os that eat the page

Atari Breakout

Google in 1998

Play Pac-Man Doodle

Zerg Rush

A Great Place to Work

Google has offices in more than 40 countries! It often tops the list of the best companies to work for. People who work for Google are called Googlers.

Google offices are often colorful and fun. Some offices have special features that reflect their country or location. For example, Googlers in the Switzerland office can hold meetings in gondolas. In Amsterdam, the café ceiling looks like Dutch waffle cookies. Googlers in Israel's office can relax at picnic tables under indoor trees.

gondolas in Switzerland office

Big As Life
Stan, a life-sized Tyrannosaurus Rex statue, stands outside of Google's headquarters!

No matter the location, Googlers enjoy special benefits. On-site cafés often serve free food and drinks. Many offices have game rooms, complete with pool and foosball tables. Some have rock climbing walls and putting greens! Visitors may even find four-legged friends walking the halls. Googlers are welcome to bring their dogs to work.

Google Gives Back

In 2004, Google started an organization called Google.org. The organization gives $100 million to local and global programs each year. Many seek to improve health care and the environment. One program has a **crisis response** team. The team helps by creating maps for people to easily find shelter and information.

Google.org also supports education. It provides technology and training for teachers and students around the world. Google.org gives away $1 billion worth of products every year!

Google employees support their communities in other ways. Thousands of Googlers help at different organizations. Together, they **volunteer** around 80,000 hours each year. Many Googlers teach technology skills. Others build homes, prepare meals, or plant trees. Through technology and people power, Google is changing the world for the better.

Google Science Fair

Google encourages young scientists. The company hosts an online science fair for teenagers each year. Students from around the world enter their projects to win prizes.

Don't Be Evil
Google motto

Googlers
volunteering

Google Timeline

1995
Larry Page and Sergey Brin meet at Stanford University in Palo Alto, California

2005
Google buys Android Inc.

2004
Google moves to a campus called the Googleplex in Mountain View, California

1998
Google Inc. becomes a company

2004
Gmail and Google.org are launched

1996
Larry and Sergey release their first search engine, BackRub, at Stanford University

1999
Google opens offices in Mountain View, California

2005
Google Maps and Google Earth are released

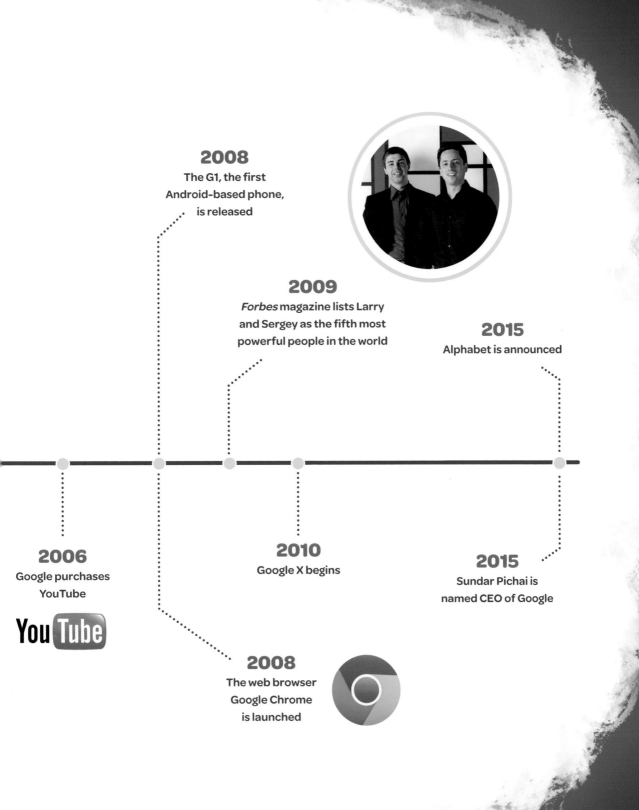

2008

The G1, the first
Android-based phone,
is released

2009

Forbes magazine lists Larry
and Sergey as the fifth most
powerful people in the world

2015

Alphabet is announced

2006

Google purchases
YouTube

2010

Google X begins

2015

Sundar Pichai is
named CEO of Google

2008

The web browser
Google Chrome
is launched

Glossary

advertise—to announce or promote something to get people to buy it

app—a small, specialized program downloaded onto computers, smartphones, or other devices

backlinks—incoming links from web pages to other web sites; backlinks determine how popular a web site will be.

brands—categories of products all made by the same company

CEO—Chief Executive Officer; the CEO is the highest-ranking person in a company.

crisis response—people trained to help victims of disasters

data mining—using computers to collect information and then looking for meaningful patterns hidden within it

founders—the people who created a company

googol—the mathematical term for a one followed by 100 zeros, or 10^{100}

headquarters—a company's main office

investment—to put money into something with hopes that it will provide financial profit

operating system—the main program in a mobile device that controls the way it works; an operating system makes it possible for other programs to function.

search engine—a program that collects and organizes information from the Internet

software—a program that tells a computer what to do

tablets—handheld computers

thermostats—devices that control indoor temperatures

virtual reality—a pretend 3D world containing sights and sounds created by computers

volunteer—to do something for others without expecting money in return

web—an information system on the Internet that allows content to be linked to other content; web is short for World Wide Web.

web browser—a software program that allows users to find and read information

To Learn More

AT THE LIBRARY

Green, Sara. *Larry Page*. Minneapolis, Minn.: Bellwether Media, 2015.

Green, Sara. *Sergey Brin*. Minneapolis, Minn.: Bellwether Media, 2015.

Ventura, Marne. *Google Glass and Robotics Innovator Sebastian Thrun*. Minneapolis, Minn.: Lerner Publications, 2014.

ON THE WEB

Learning more about Google is as easy as 1, 2, 3.

1. Go to www.factsurfer.com.

2. Enter "Google" into the search box.

3. Click the "Surf" button and you will see a list of related web sites.

With factsurfer.com, finding more information is just a click away.

Index

The images in this book are reproduced through the courtesy of: juniorbeep, front cover (Android); Robert Fruehauf, front cover (Chromecast Stick); Asif Islam, front cover (Venture logo), p. 12 (bottom); Alexander Supertramp, front cover (Gmail icon, Google Chrome logo, Google+ logo); Bloomua, front cover (Gmail logo, Nexus phone, Google Play logo), p. 4 (top); Mahathir Mohd Yasin, front cover (Waze logo); Spauln, front cover (Google Play card); Em7, front cover (Street View icon); r.nagy, front cover (Google Wallet logo); Twin Design, front cover (Google Maps logo, Blogger logo); DibaniMedia, front cover (Nexus phone back); Petar Chernaev, front cover (Nexus tablet, Nexus tablet small); 360b, front cover (YouTube logo); Mopic, front cover (Google Glass); Bizoon, front cover (Picasa logo); rvlsoft, pp. 3, 4 (bottom left); Alexey Boldin, pp. 4 (bottom right), 10 (bottom), 20 (bottom); SiliconValleyStock/ Alamy, p. 5; Your Design, p. 6; SuperStock/ Glow Images, pp. 7, 21 (top); Aerial Archives/ Alamy, p. 8; sjscreens/ Alamy, p. 9; Rose Carson, pp. 10 (top), 21 (bottom left, bottom right); Modfos, p. 11 (top); Iain Masterton/ Alamy, p. 11 (bottom); Hugh Threlfall/ Alamy, p. 12 (top); Robin Beckham/ BEEPstock/ Alamy, p. 13 (top); Alexandru Nika, p. 13 (bottom); Albert Gea/ Reuters/ Corbis, p. 14 (top); Martial Red, p. 14 (bottom); Juan Martinez, pp. 15, 20; Walter Bieri/ EPA/ Newscom, p. 16; John Gilbey/ Alamy, p. 17; Steve Jennings/ Getty Images, p. 19; turtix, p. 20 (top).